D0088442

Staying Strong
Real-Life Stories About Teens

by Christina Cheakalos, Lyndon Stambler,
Christy Damio, Jonathan Blum, Marc Aronoff,
Laura D'Angelo, and Karen Fanning

SCHOLASTIC INC.
New York Toronto London Auckland Sydney
Mexico City New Delhi Hong Kong Buenos Aires

Cover Photo:
Aniak Volunteer Fire Department
Back Cover Photos:
L to R: © Brent Stirton/Liaison/Getty Images;
© Barbara Grover Photography;
© Jason Tanaka Blaney;
© Darren McCollester/Liaison/Getty Images.

Contents

The Dragon Slayers are great friends off the job, and hard-working crewmates on the job.

1 The Dragon Slayers

In the wilds of Alaska, these teenage girls could be your only hope!

It's 10:20 A.M. in Aniak, Alaska. It's spring. The temperature is 20 degrees. And there's blinding snow! Volunteer Fire Chief Pete Brown radios his team. He tells them to meet him at George Peterson's home. Peterson is an elderly man. It is hard for him to breathe.

Minutes later, Brown and his team are there. "What's wrong with me?" asks Peterson. "It hurts."

"We're going to give you some oxygen," Dione Turner tells him. She has a soothing voice. "It will make you feel better," promises Patty Yaska. Patty hooks him up to an oxygen tank.

Soon, Peterson feels better. He chats with his rescuers. And he notices that they are very young.

Patty and Dione, both 17, leave. Peterson turns to his son Ray, who made the 911 call. "Who were those girls?" he asks. Ray replies. "They're the Dragon Slayers."

To the Rescue!

The Dragon Slayers are a team of seven high-school girls. They are volunteer emergency medical technicians (EMTs). Each girl has had 200 hours of training. They provide 24-hour emergency medical care. Sometimes it's the only care available to 3,000 people in 14 villages. The team covers an area the size of Maryland. They respond to 450 calls a year.

Erinn Marteney is the youngest Dragon Slayer. She is 14. She pulled a toddler from a fire. Team members have saved villagers who fell through ice. They have revived heart attack victims. They have helped snowmobilers hurt in accidents. They have rescued survivors of small-plane crashes. "It really changes how you are as a person." That's what Erica Kameroff, 16, says.

The area is remote. Most people who live there are Yupik Eskimos and Athabascan Indians. Getting to victims is a challenge. No roads connect the town to the rest of Alaska. It is surrounded by rivers. But the team knows the area well. They live here too. Frozen waterways are their highways. The team uses snowmobiles. Or they use four-wheel-drive vehicles. In warmer months, the ice melts. Then they use boats.

Critical Condition

Pete Brown is a Vietnam vet. He has extensive EMT training. He created the Dragon Slayers in 1993. It was the day after his son Jeremiah was hit by a four-wheeler. Jeremiah hurt his legs and broke his hands. He lay in the snow for 45 minutes. That's how long it took for help to come.

"There was no health care after 4 P.M.," says Brown. Aniak had no ambulance.

The village finally got a medical clinic two years later. But a doctor only comes once a month. "We are blessed to have these girls," says Victoria Hazard. She is a nurse at the clinic. "They are very professional. This saves me time when the patient gets here."

Grace Bender saw the Dragon Slayers' skills up close. Her husband, Chuck, had a stroke. "They went to work," says Bender. "Nobody raised their voice. Everyone was efficient. Every time I see them now, my heart smiles."

Intensive Care

The girls feel committed to each other and Chief Brown, too. Their chief is a 6'4" carpenter. He built the local fire station by hand. "The thing I like about Pete is that he listens," says Patty Yaska. "When you need to talk, he'll drop everything."

After Jeremiah's accident, Brown held rescue training classes. People came. The adults gradually quit, though. They had other commitments. After five years of service, the boys also dropped out. They preferred hunting and snowboarding. They didn't want to do rescue work. So the Dragon Slayers became an all-girl team. "Dragon Slayers" is a nickname for firefighters. Jeremiah had read about the nickname in a magazine. He liked it.

Brown has strict rules. Members must attend weekly training meetings. They must get passing grades in school. They must be alcohol- and drug-free. The girls also care for elderly residents. This helps them gain experience.

Twice a week for three years, the Dragon Slayers cared for Hugo Olson. He had lung disease. Their duty ended when he died. He was 75. "Hugo taught them not only the techniques of medicine," says Brown. "He taught the generosity of giving and the sweet sting of compassion."

Medical Attention

The team was getting noticed. The Aniak Volunteer Fire Department was honored in 1995. They were called the best ambulance service in Alaska.

Hollywood has also been paying attention. There might be a TV series. If a pilot is made, the group will get $75,000. It will go to a scholarship fund.

This money could help boost the girls' dreams. Fauna Morris hopes to attend the University of Alaska. She wants to be a pediatrician. The chief's daughter is Mariah Brown. She wants to be a rescue swimmer. Patty wants to be a flight paramedic. Kimberly Gregory plans to join the Air Force.

A younger group is ready to take over. There's one boy, too. They are now in training. They are called the Lizard Killers. When will they be ready to become Dragon Slayers? That's up to Brown.

Meanwhile, the current Dragon Slayers haven't let fame go to their heads. They hang out at the fire station. They do homework. They dance with "Choking Charlie." That's the mannequin they use to practice rescues.

Then their beepers go off. They're on the move. "This has given them self-confidence," says Brown. "The outside world isn't going to scare these girls."

2 Coping With Tragedy

Brittany Chevalier lost her brother in the September 11th attacks. She and other teens came together to cope.

On September 11, 2001, 34 people from Middletown, New Jersey died. They were victims of the World Trade Center attacks. One of those killed was Brittany Chevalier's brother. How did Brittany cope? She started a support group for teens.

A Special Bond

Brittany's parents split up when she was in fifth grade. Her dad moved out. Brittany's brother Swede, 21, became the man of the family. Swede came home from college. "That's when my brother and I became really good friends," Brittany remembers.

Swede was more than a friend to Brittany. "He was like a father figure," she says. "My brother was a big part of my life."

Swede was close to his mother and his other sister, Tylia, too. He worked at the World Trade Center. It was in nearby New York City.

On the night of September 10, 2001, Swede came home from work. The siblings chatted. "I think God gave me a feeling," says Brittany. "When we were talking my heart filled up with love for my brother. I gave him a hug and a kiss. Then I went and did my homework."

Later, Brittany passed Swede's room. She was on her way to bed. They said goodnight. Brittany switched off his light and left the room.

A Tragic Loss

That was the last time Brittany saw her brother. The next morning, two airplanes hit the World Trade Center. The buildings were destroyed.

"I was in third-period biology," Brittany recalls. "The kid next to me said to my teacher, 'Did you know a plane crashed into the World Trade

**"My brother was the strongest person I ever knew,"
says Brittany.**

© Jason Tanaka Blaney

Center?'" The principal made the same announcement a few minutes later.

Brittany's mom came to the school. She took Brittany home. Tylia came home from college. The family waited for news.

"It was such a beautiful day," Brittany recalls. "I remember sitting outside smelling the smoke. It was going right over my head."

Swede's body was found three days later.

A Time to Mourn

Brittany stayed home from school for two weeks. She had a lot of work to make up when she returned. Sometimes it was hard to focus. Life without Swede was very different. Often it was very sad.

Brittany had love and support from her family. She had sympathy from her neighbors. Rock stars even performed a benefit concert for victims' families. But sharing her feelings with other teens helped her the most.

"They say that teens grieve differently from adults," said Brittany. "Their grief turns on and off.

I agree with that. One minute I'll be fine. An hour later I'll be miserable."

A Place to Go

Brittany talked with her friend Brad. He had lost his father. They'd both noticed many support groups for adults. "We decided that we needed one for teens," Brittany remembers.

In November, they were ready to invite others to join. They had a dinner. Teens who had been affected were invited. Now, the members meet regularly. They socialize. They don't always discuss September 11th. But they feel comfortable talking about it together.

The group members also reach out. They help families affected by the disaster. They wrap holiday presents. They baby-sit.

Helping others makes Brittany feel better. And talking about Swede helps too. "It's still very hard," she says. "But I like to remember him."

3 *Battling Dyslexia*

**He couldn't play sports. He couldn't read.
And no one knew why.**

For years, Dustin Hunter dreaded school. Even in kindergarten, he struggled to keep up.

"I almost didn't get to go on to first grade. I couldn't skip," Dustin, now 13, recalls.

Dustin watched other kids play sports in his hometown of Gold Beach, Oregon. He found sports impossible.

"At my school, popularity was based on sports," Dustin says. "My eyes didn't focus right. So I didn't play sports well. I lost a lot of friends."

By first grade, sports weren't Dustin's only problem. He was having trouble learning to read.

"It was stressful," Dustin remembers. "It took an hour to read a simple page."

Stress at School

Dustin's parents tried to help. His teachers tried to help. But no one could figure out what was wrong. He did well in math. Yet reading was a struggle.

"It was frustrating," Dustin remembers. "Most kids would finish their homework in less than an hour. I would spend all night working with my mom. But I would forget what I'd learned by the next night. I couldn't hold it."

Meanwhile, school was hard for Dustin socially. He was called names. He got bullied.

By sixth grade, Dustin's teachers said that he wasn't doing well enough in the regular classroom. He was reading at a second grade level. He was put in a special education class.

Looking for Answers

Dustin's parents searched outside of school for answers. They took him to a clinic. There, Dustin took some tests. He was diagnosed with a learning disability called dyslexia.

Dyslexia is a disorder of the brain. It often affects reading, writing, and spelling.

Dustin had trouble keeping his eyes focused on words. He had perfect vision. But his eyes couldn't focus for more than a few seconds. Then the image would blur.

Dustin and his parents were relieved. They finally knew what was happening. But coping with the disability was hard work for Dustin.

He had to exercise his eyes every day. But he was determined. He completed a two-year course at the clinic. It only took him six months!

Back at school, things didn't get easier right away. Dustin still got bullied.

"We went to the police a couple of times," Dustin recalls. "Some kids kept punching me."

But his self-confidence was growing. He knew he could do better in school.

Do-Over

Seventh grade finally ended. Dustin made a big decision. He asked to repeat the grade.

© Timothy Bullard Photography/Zapature Agency

Dustin worked hard to overcome his learning disability.

"I thought if I got held back," he says, "I would lose some of the people who were mean to me. I could also catch up on all the years I'd missed. I think it's been a wise decision."

It has. Now Dustin's back full-time in a regular classroom. His reading scores have jumped. He does better at sports. And his grades have improved a lot. He's close to making honor roll.

Dustin's also happier with his social life. "I have better friends," he says.

Dustin has also found a new hobby. It's chess. He has a talent for it.

"I enjoy the challenge," he says. "I like seeing how many ways I can trick people into falling into traps."

Dustin wants to forget the hard times. But he'll always remember what got him through those years. He respected himself, no matter what.

4 My Tough Choice: Jail or Boot Camp

This teen was headed for trouble. Would boot camp set her straight?

Stacy was skipping school almost every day. "I fell in with the wrong crowd," she says. Her mom tried to get her to behave. But Stacy ignored her. She fought with other students. She got in trouble with the law. Stacy had to make a choice. "Either I was going to a boot camp or to jail." Stacy chose boot camp.

Testing the Limits

Teens at boot camp get treated like they are in the army. It's not like summer camp. There is no canoeing. Nobody sings campfire songs. They had to run four miles every morning at 4:00. "I often woke up feeling cold and dirty," Stacy recalls.

Stacy made a decision that turned her life around. In the background, her counselor and mom look on.

For most of the day, they did tough outdoor activities. They went hiking. They went rock climbing. They went rope climbing. At night they slept in tents. They were only allowed three showers per week.

Rope-climbing was the hardest part for Stacy. "Sometimes I had to climb up 50 feet or more," she remembers. Each time Stacy met a challenge, she got stronger physically. She got stronger mentally, too.

Talking it Over

Every day, the girls had group counseling. At first Stacy hated talking about her problems in front of others. She told her group leaders that the whole idea was stupid. But she was really just embarrassed. "I thought others might laugh at me," Stacy admits.

Finally Stacy shared with the group. No one made fun of her. "I became more open about my feelings," she says. She told them about her mom. She talked about her anger.

Stacy learned ways to cope with her problems. Now she can control her anger. She counts to ten. "This helps me blow off steam. I think twice before saying something hurtful."

Making Changes

The campers were told to write letters to important people in their lives. Stacy wrote to her mom. She felt bad about the mean things she had said and done to her. Stacy realized something important. "My mom was trying to control my temper because she loved me."

One night, Stacy was lying awake. She decided that things would change at home. She would show her mom more respect.

Stacy is striving to keep that promise. She's working hard to have a good relationship with her mom. She's staying out of trouble. She sees a counselor. This helps her think about her problems so she can deal with them. "In some ways, boot camp was the worst experience of my life," Stacy says. "But I also learned a lot about myself."

5 *Miro the Hero*

Miro Legin lost his legs in a land mine accident when he was 13 years old. But that hasn't slowed him down.

In November 2001, Miroslav Legin entered the New York City Marathon. It was his second year in a row. He covered the 26.2-mile distance in one hour, 52 minutes. He got a medal! About 30,000 people run the marathon every year. But Miro stood out. The 19-year-old competed on a special bike. It's called a hand cycle. He pedaled with his hands because he has no legs.

A Country at War

Miro had a typical childhood. He grew up in Sarajevo. It's a city in the Eastern European country of Bosnia and Herzegovina. He was like many kids. Miro loved his family. He enjoyed sports and games. He played with his friends.

Bosnia went to war in 1992. Miro was ten. Times were hard. He and his brother had to work. They hauled wood for neighbors. Miro remembers, "They'd only give us two bucks each. But we were surviving."

An Innocent Victim

The war ended on December 14, 1995. Many people were left poor. But life slowly began to go back to normal. For Miro, however, more changes were on the way.

Six months later, Miro was walking near the front lines. That's where most of the fighting had happened. People didn't know it, but there were still some land mines around. A land mine is a small bomb buried in the ground. A mine exploded beneath Miro's feet.

Miro survived. But his legs didn't.

He spent 55 days in the hospital. Miro also went to Germany several times. He got more treatment

© Brent Stirton/Getty Images

"Some people treat me like a kid because I'm in a wheelchair. That bothers me a lot," Miro says. Here, he practices on his hand cycle.

there. It was hard traveling to another country alone. "Nobody spoke my language," Miro recalls.

People asked Miro how he'd lost his legs. "It's a small thing," he told them. "It's the size of a burger. And it can ruin your life."

A New Opportunity

But Miro wouldn't let the land mine ruin his life. He knew that with the right help he could have a full and happy life.

In September of 2000, Miro went to New York City for more treatment. There he met Dick Traum. He was the president and founder of the Achilles Track Club. This group is made up of physically challenged athletes. They compete in races. Some use wheelchairs. Others use hand cycles. Dick told Miro about the New York City Marathon.

The race was only a few weeks away. Miro had no experience. He asked Dick how long the race might take him. Dick said, "I think it'll take you four hours."

Miro finished the 26.2-mile race in two hours, 38 minutes. He beat many other racers. He even beat Dick. The next year, Dick sent Miro an invitation to the same race. Miro trained hard. He did even better than before.

A Plan for the Future

By age 19, Miro was getting used to life in a wheelchair. He had even become an athlete. But his life still isn't easy. "I have a hard time when I see my friends playing sports you need legs for," he says.

Miro knows he's come a long way since he was injured. Now he has new goals to pursue. He wants to settle in New York. Life there is easier for people in wheelchairs. He also has career goals. "If I ever get a chance, I'll be a New York City cop," Miro says.

Police officers have to be determined. They have to be brave. Miro has shown both qualities.

6 Fitting In

This teen's first report card in an American school was nothing to brag about. It had two F's and a D. By the time she graduated from high school, she had an A average.

Irene, 18, was born in Puebla, Mexico. "I have good memories of my childhood," Irene says.

"I had cousins to play with," she recalls. Irene also had her mother, grandmother, and younger sister. But her father lived in Los Angeles. It was far away.

Irene's parents wanted a good education for their girls. But school expenses in Mexico were higher than the family could afford. So Irene's family moved to Los Angeles when she was nine.

Irene will never forget how hard it was. She had

to say goodbye to her grandmother. "I remember it as clearly as if it was two days ago," Irene says. "She waved good-bye. It was so hard to look back and see her."

Home Sweet Home?

Irene was happy to see her father in Los Angeles. But moving was a big change. There had been lots of open space in Mexico. There were no freeways or streetlights there. Now she was in a huge, crowded city. "I felt like I was in a different world. I was lost," Irene remembers.

Irene entered fifth grade. She could only speak a few English words. She got two F's and a D on her first report card. Her father was upset. "He told me 'I'm not sending you to school to get this type of grade,'" Irene remembers. "After that, I made it my goal to get straight A's."

High-Rise

Irene was doing better by ninth grade. She became more confident with her English. "Before, I couldn't even stand being in class. I would blush.

Besides clothes, these two photographs are all Irene brought with her when she moved to L.A. They are pictures of her grandparents.

I would feel my head boiling," Irene remembers. "As time passed, I learned to speak in front of a class. I learned how to have a conversation."

Irene also started volunteering. She joined groups. She followed her interests in medicine, business, graphic arts, and public speaking.

The On-Ramp

Irene joined a program called OnRamp Arts. She writes and designs online games.

In the games, players go on quests. They try to reach a goal. Irene and her classmates use personal stories to design the quests. They also use their imaginations and Latin American history.

Irene and her group designed a game called *Making of the Delicious Tamale*. The game follows the adventure of a girl, Leecha. She explores her roots to find out how to make a tamale. A tamale is a Mexican treat. It tastes like cornbread.

Irene says the creative projects that teens have accomplished at OnRamp show what they can do. It helps break stereotypes about Hispanic teens in L.A.

"We are showing that we are capable of doing this. Give us a chance," she says. "OnRamp Arts gives us the opportunity to create our own stories."

College-Bound

Irene's next big challenge is affording college. She plans to study business and graphic arts. She knows it will be expensive. But she's going to do everything in her power to make it happen.

Irene has some advice for immigrants. "If you're an immigrant, a lot of things get in your way," Irene says. "Always look at them not as obstacles, but as challenges."

7 Looking Out for Family

Chris Patche has always looked out for his family. That's because he's the only one in the family who can see.

When he was five years old, Chris Patche of Sacramento, California, made an amazing discovery. Not all parents are blind.

Chris is the only person in his family with full sight. He assumed all families were just like his. Then a new neighbor invited Chris to his house.

"We were playing with his race car track. His mother walked in. She asked me if I wanted something to drink. She made eye contact with me. And I wondered if she could see me," Chris says.

Then Chris moved around the room. He watched the woman follow him with her eyes.

"I couldn't believe it," says Chris, who's now 15. It took a while for the discovery to sink in.

"It made me feel bad. For the first time I realized I was different. But I got over that."

Keeping an Eye on Things

Chris's mother, Joni, has been blind since birth. His father, Paul Sr., was born without irises. Irises are the colored parts around the pupils. Chris's 14-year-old brother Paul was born without irises too. So was his ten-year-old sister, Robin. They can see rough outlines. But they can't make out details.

"They can see where you are, but maybe not who you are," Joni says.

With the sharpest vision in the house, Chris always helps out. He and his mother go grocery shopping. Chris picks out the vegetables. The family watches movies together. Chris describes what's happening during the silent scenes.

"I've always helped people find things. I used to run around looking for my brother's and sister's shoes. I'd tell them if their shirts didn't match their pants," Chris says.

All children test their parents. Chris came up with unique tricks. At age four, he tried to watch

© Thor Swift

Chris is happy to help his family members.

The Patche family goes for a walk.

© Thor Swift

more TV than his parents allowed. Once he turned on cartoons without the sound.

"I knew right away," Joni says, laughing. "He wasn't listening to a word I said. He didn't answer even when I asked him if he was watching TV."

Chris disobeys his parents once in a while, Joni says. But she trusts him.

"Chris is a really honest kid. He could deceive us. But he tells the truth," she says.

Meet the Parents

Joni appreciates Chris's help. Still, she doesn't want him to feel responsible for the family.

"I knew that when I had kids, I was not going to depend on them to tell me what the traffic is like. I'm an independent person. I don't need to ask," she says. "Sometimes I'll ask Chris if my shirt looks all right. I won't know if the coffee I spilled came out in the wash. But I try not to interrupt him if he's busy."

Chris says he doesn't mind helping. But he is also proud of the way his parents take care of themselves. His mother used to come to his class. She brought her guide dog. She would read Braille books to the class.

"The kids thought it was cool," Chris says. "They'd ask, 'How can she read those little bumps?'"

At the house, friends would ask questions. They'd ask how his parents got to the store. (They walk.) They'd ask how his parents found things in the cupboard. (They make Braille labels.)

"It used to bother me if they'd stare. They'd

watch my mom go to the fridge. I'd say, 'What are you looking at? She's not going to do anything weird,'" Chris says. "My parents would laugh."

Away from Home

Chris now goes to a smaller high school. It's an hour away from his parents' house. During the week, he stays with his grandmother. She lives near the school. On weekends, he goes home and spends time with the family.

"Being away can be hard. I start missing my family," Chris says.

Sometimes he worries. Maybe his parents will lose something valuable, like a wedding ring. They would have to wait for him to come home and find it. But, Chris says, "They manage fine without me."

8 Fighting for My Life

At first, Rebecca Karp thought she had pulled a muscle in her leg. It turned out to be a rare, fast-growing cancer. Rebecca was forced to look death in the eye at age 15. She fought back. This is her story.

A month into my freshman year, I was still really excited about starting high school. I was signed up to play field hockey. I was making new friends. But my life was about to change forever.

Diagnosis: Cancer

When the doctor told me he thought I had cancer, I was shocked. I thought to myself, "Cancer? I barely know what it is." I had never known anyone with cancer. All I knew was that people die from it.

I was scared. So was my family. My mom and I just sat in the waiting room and cried.

I got home. My brothers were outside playing hockey. One brother asked, "Do you really have cancer?" It was obvious that he didn't know anything about it either. I said "Yeah." I walked into the house. I felt stunned.

My mom had called my grandmother from the hospital. She was at the house when I got home. My grandmother hugged me. She said, "It's going to be long. But we'll get through it." I didn't want to think about it. I just lay down on the couch and stared at the ceiling.

Later, my dad came home. He was crying as he sat down next to me. He hugged me. He said he was sorry. Everyone was sorry. And none of us knew what would happen next.

That night, I called my best friend, Lauren. She had called earlier. My grandmother had told her it didn't look good. So Lauren was really nervous. I just told her it was cancer. We could barely talk. We sat on the phone and listened to each other cry.

© Darren McCollester/Getty Images

Rebecca's life changed when she found out she had a deadly disease.

A few days later, test results confirmed what the doctor had said. I had to start chemotherapy treatment two weeks later.

No Choice But to Fight

The first time I got chemo, they gave me antinausea medicine. But the next morning I was really sick anyway. I threw up. I felt bad. It lasted for a couple of days. My mom took care of me. But there was not much anyone could do.

The second time it was even worse. I couldn't keep any food down for an entire week. I lost ten pounds. I felt so weak. It was ironic. The cure was what was making me feel so sick. The medicines of chemo have to be strong enough to kill cancer cells. So I knew I didn't have a choice. I had to fight for my life.

Losing My Hair

As time went on, I didn't get as sick. But I started losing my hair. In some ways, that was worse. It was really gross. Standing in the shower, I watched tons of it sliding off my head. It collected

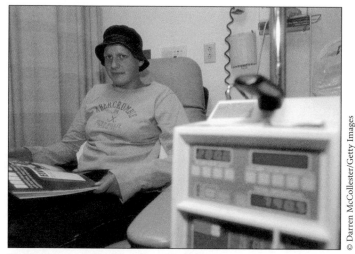

Rebecca received chemotherapy.

around the drain. It was all over my pillow. It was all over my clothes. I begged my mom not to make me go to school. She thought it would keep things normal. I felt like things would never be normal.

I became depressed. Every day my hair was getting thinner. Every time I looked in the mirror, I cried. Finally, I let my neighbor Matt shave my head for me. That was a turning point.

Back to School

Once I shaved my head, I felt better. I thought it was cool not having hair. I kind of liked it.

I started going back to school. I wore bandanas for a while. Then I wore hats. At school, most kids were normal to me. They didn't treat me any differently. But there were some kids who didn't know what to say or do. I didn't care. If they wanted to ask questions, I wasn't offended. I'd answer them.

It was tough to see all my friends at school. They knew how hard it was for me. I would often be out for a whole week after the chemo. It made me feel so sick. My friend Lauren had a really hard time handling it. Yet she was right by my side whenever I needed her. And, she always came over to drop off my homework. My friend Megan has a different personality. She was always upbeat. She got me in a good mood. She really stuck by me, too.

Life After Cancer

I missed a lot of my freshman year during those months of chemotherapy. I missed a lot of class work. I didn't get to meet many of my classmates.

I wasn't in school enough to make new friends. And I couldn't do sports. I wasn't strong enough.

On August 1, 2000, I finished my rounds of chemotherapy and radiation treatments.

My doctors continue to monitor me and give me tests. Sometimes I think about what could happen if my cancer comes back. It's still in the back of my mind. But I try not to dwell on it.

My family and friends gave me a lot of strength, hope, and courage to get me through this. But I also found those things within myself.

I value life a lot more now. I'm positive that I'm going to live to be as old as anyone else.